What's New at the Zoo?

An Animal Adding Adventure

By Suzanne Slade

Illustrated by Joan Waites

Let's go on an animal adventure,
how many live in the zoo?
We'll add up each creature —
moms, dads, and their new babies, too!

Two hungry pandas
eat a bamboo lunch.
One cub joins the meal.
How many crunch and munch?

Four dusty elephants
spraying water jets —
two calves join the fun.
How many getting wet?

4 + 2 = ?

Two tiny peachicks
gather round peahen.
Add one papa peacock.
How many in the pen?

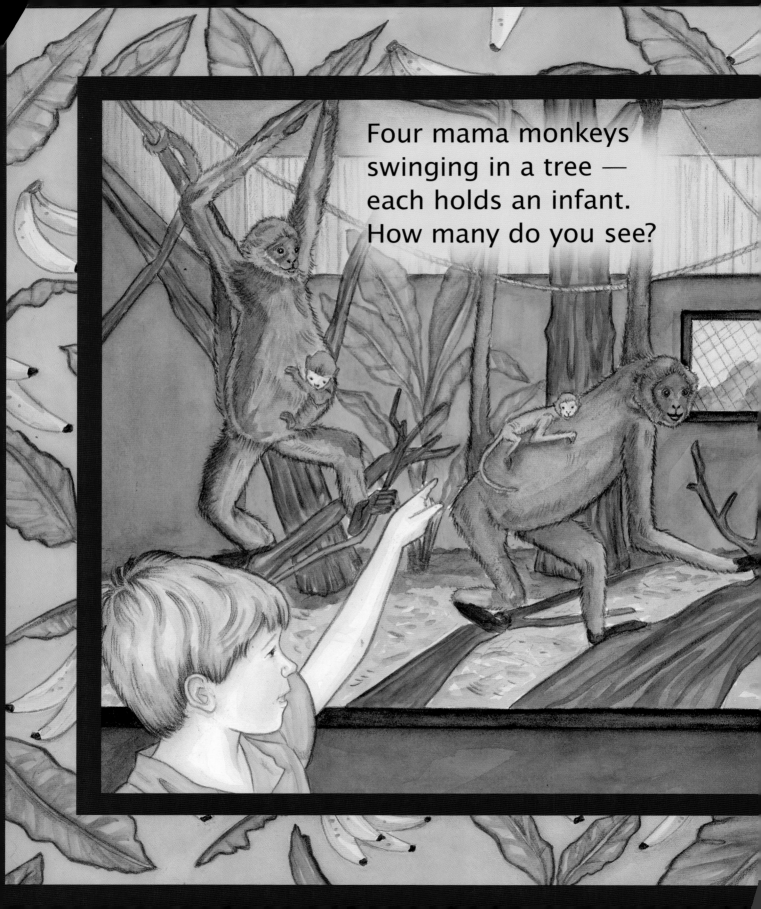

Four mama monkeys
swinging in a tree —
each holds an infant.
How many do you see?

Three mammoth boas
plus two neonates
loop around the branches.
How many figure eights?

5 + 2 = ?

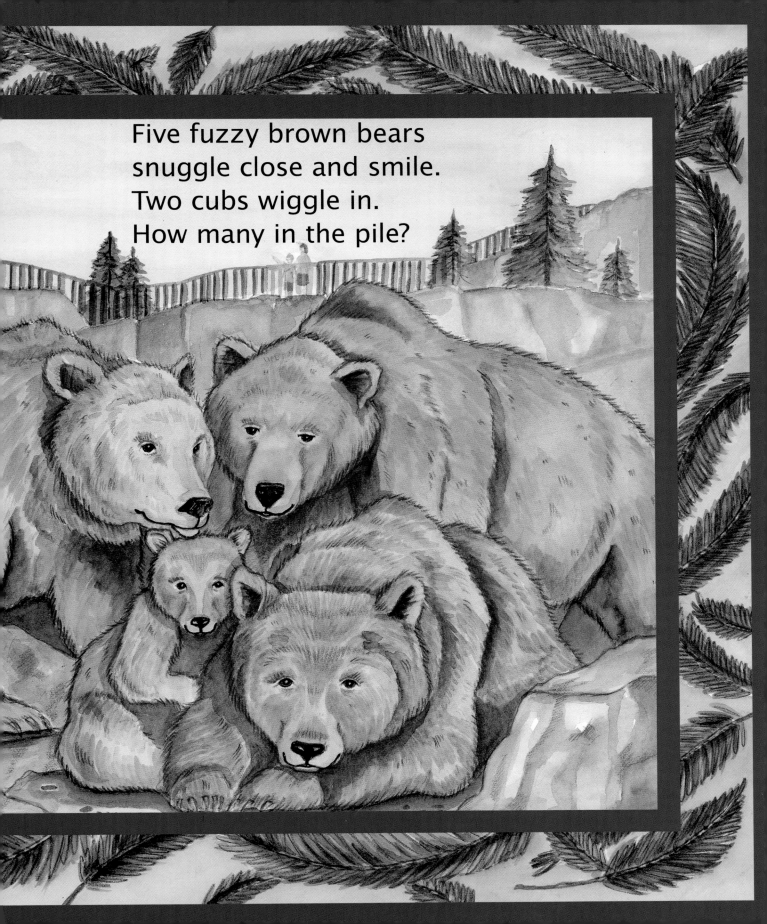

Five fuzzy brown bears
snuggle close and smile.
Two cubs wiggle in.
How many in the pile?

5+4 = ?

Five boomers bouncing
up and down non-stop.
Four jumping joeys join.
How many like to hop?

Six speedy zebras
run their fastest pace.
Four foals trot behind.
How many in the race?

Eight spotted long necks
stretching straight and tall —
five calves cuddle close.
What's the sum of all?

Ten playful penguins
slip and slide and flip.
Five chicks want a turn.
How many take a dip?

10 + 5 = ?

12 + 8 = ?

Twelve hanging fruit bats
sleeping sound and deep —
eight pups hide under wings.
How many are asleep?

$+ 4 = 8$

$3 + 2 = 5$

$5 + 4 = 9$

$2 + 1 = 3$

$+ 5 = 15$

Our math adventure is nearly done.
We saw many creatures at play.
Adding animals is lots of fun!
How many did we find today?

For Creative Minds

How Many Animals Did You See at the Zoo?

Addition Method I: Tens Make Friends

One way to find the total of many numbers is to arrange the numbers into groups that add up to multiples of ten. For example, 3 + 7 = 10. It's easier to add up tens and find the grand total.

Group 1: **3** pandas + **7** bears = **10** animals	10 animals
Group 2: **6** elephants + **4** peafowl = **10** animals	10 animals
Group 3: **15** penguins + **5** snakes = **20** animals	20 animals
Group 4: **8** monkeys + **9** kangaroos + **13** giraffes = **30** animals	30 animals
Group 5: **10** zebras + **20** bats = **30** animals	+ 30 animals
	100 animals

Addition Method II: Adding by Columns

When adding many numbers, you can also add the numbers in the ones column first. A number that has only one numeral is in the ones column. If a number is made of two numbers (13, for example), then the number to the right, (in this case the 3) is in the ones column.

3 Pandas
4 Peafowl
5 Snakes
6 Elephants
7 Bears
8 Monkeys
9 Kangaroos
10 Zebras
13 Giraffes
15 Penguins
20 Bats

First, add the numbers in the ones column:
3 + 4 + 5 + 6 + 7 + 8 + 9 + 0 + 3 + 5 + 0 = 50
The total from the ones column = 50 animals

Next, add the numbers in the tens column: 1 + 1 + 1 + 2 = 5
Five tens means the total in the tens column = 50 animals

Now add the totals from the ones and tens column together to find the grand total.

+ **50** animals from the ones column
   50 animals from the tens column
_____
100 animals at the zoo!

Adding it All Up — Fact Families

Just as animals in a family are related to each other, numbers in a fact family are related too. The three numbers in each fact family below are related to each other by the four math facts beside them.

4 elephants + ? elephants = 6 elephants
2 elephants + 4 elephants = ? elephants
6 elephants - 4 elephants = ? elephants
? elephants - 2 elephants = 4 elephants

4

2   **6**

8

5   **13**

8 giraffes + ? giraffes = 13 giraffes
5 giraffes + 8 giraffes = ? giraffes
13 giraffes - 5 giraffes = ? giraffes
? giraffes - 8 giraffes = 5 giraffes

4 zebras + ? zebras = 10 zebras
6 zebras + 4 zebras = ? zebras
10 zebras - 4 zebras = ? zebras
? zebras - 6 zebras = 4 zebras

4

6   **10**

2

1   **3**

2 pandas + ? pandas = 3 pandas
1 panda + 2 pandas = ? pandas
3 pandas - 2 pandas = ? pandas
? pandas - 1 panda = 2 pandas

4 kangaroos + ? kangaroos = 9 kangaroos
5 kangaroos + 4 kangaroos = ? kangaroos
9 kangaroos - 4 kangaroos = ? kangaroos
? kangaroos - 5 kangaroos = 4 kangaroos

4

5   **9**

Animal Matching Activity

Many animals are called by a special name when they are babies. Each animal baby is unique and develops differently. See if you can match the baby animal description to its picture. Answers are upside down at the bottom of the page.

1. These **cubs** are about the size of a pet hamster, are blind, and don't have any fur or teeth when born. The mother stays in her safe, cozy den with her baby cubs for about a month. Young cubs drink milk from their mothers. When they are about a year old, cubs begin eating tender leaves from bamboo plants. Later, after their teeth become strong enough to chew, they will also eat the tough bamboo stems.

A.

2. Newborn **calves** weigh about 250 pounds (113 kg)! These huge babies are able to stand soon after they are born. These calves drink milk from their mothers. When they are a few months old, calves begin to munch on grass. These babies like to follow their mothers wherever they go. They might even suck on their trunks much like young children suck their thumbs!

B.

3. These colorful animals are related to pheasants. The males are called peacocks and are well-known for their long, beautiful tails. The females are called peahens, but their feathers are not as brightly colored as the peacocks. In the spring, peahens lay a group of seven to ten brown eggs. About 30 days later, tiny peachicks hatch from the eggs. They are called peachicks until they are about one-year old.

C.
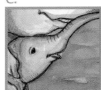

4. Some of these primate **infants** weigh about one pound (454 g) when born. These small furry creatures spend most of their time riding on their mothers' bellies or backs and drinking their milk. When they get older, they also dine on fresh fruit, leaves, or flowers. Because they live in trees, infants quickly learn how to walk across tree branches.

D.

5. A **neonate** has plenty of company because its mother gives birth to 20 to 60 neonates at a time. Neonates weigh about three ounces (85 g) when first born and are between 12 to 18 inches (30-46 cm) long. About a week later, they shed their scaly skin for the first time and begin eating and rapidly growing. Adults may weigh up to 50 pounds (23 kg) and can be 10 feet (3 m) long.

E.

6. Most females have only one baby, called a **joey**, at a time. Joeys crawl into their mothers' front pouches shortly after birth. Joeys can drink milk whenever they are hungry. Joeys usually stay snug in their mothers' pouches for about 11 months before venturing out into the world.

F.

7. **Foals** weigh around 55 pounds (25 kg) at birth. Born with their stripes, they can stand on shaky legs minutes after being born and are able to run a short distance within an hour. Foals stay near their mothers for the first few weeks. The mothers help protect their babies and give them milk when they are hungry.

G.

8. Newborn **calves** are about 6 feet (1.8 m) tall (thanks to their long necks) and usually weigh between 90 and 120 pounds (41-54 kg). Hours after being born, they are able to stand and run but spend most of their time resting near their mothers for the first two weeks. Calves drink milk from their mothers or another female "babysitter" from the herd for 9 to 12 months. They begin eating leaves when they are a few months old.

H.

9. After hatching from their eggs, these **chicks** must stay near one of their parents to keep warm. When first born, their feathers are a silky down that are later replaced by a second set of soft gray feathers. When they are about two years old, their feathers turn black and white. The feathers are covered with special waterproof oil.

I.

10. These **pups** are very tiny and may only weigh about 1 ounce (28 g) at birth. However, that could be almost 45% (almost half) of the mother's weight. That would be like a 120 pound woman giving birth to a 54 pound baby! They drink milk from their mothers. They are the only mammals that fly. Using their strong claws, newborn pups cling tightly to their mothers when they forage for food at night. During the day, pups sleep under their mothers' wings.

J.

11. Newborn **cubs** are blind and do not have any fur. The helpless cubs weigh about 18 ounces (510 g) when they are first born. The warm milk they get from their mothers helps them grow quickly. By the time they are three months old, most cubs weigh 33 pounds (15 kg). Cubs are curious creatures, but they usually don't stray too far from their mothers.

K.

Answers: 1G, 2C, 3K, 4E, 5J, 6H, 7I, 8D, 9F, 10A, 11B

Animal classes: If an animal baby drinks milk from its mother and it has hair or fur, it is a mammal. If an animal has feathers, it is a bird. Reptiles breathe oxygen from the air and have scales. Using the descriptions of each of the animals above, can you figure out which animals are mammals, birds, or reptiles? Answers are upside down below.

Matching answers:
Mammals: panda, elephant, monkey, brown bear, kangaroo, zebra, giraffe, fruit bat
Birds: peafowl, penguin
Reptile: boa constrictor

For my husband, Mike, who adds much love, excitement, and adventure to my life—SBS

To my husband Gerard, for his many years of patience and support—JW

Thanks to Mary Santilli, Presidential Award Recipient for Elementary Mathematics (CT 1991), for verifying the accuracy of the math information and to Ron Fricke, Deputy Director of the Toledo Zoo for verifying the accuracy of the animal information in the book.

Publisher's Cataloging-In-Publication Data

Slade, Suzanne.
What's new at the zoo? : an animal adding adventure / by Suzanne Slade ; illustrated by Joan Waites.

p. : col. ill. ; cm.

Summary: Travel through the zoo and learn about zoo animals through rhyme. Count up all of the animals you have seen. Includes section "For Creative Minds" with cards and activities.

Interest age level: 004-008.
Interest grade level: P-3.
Lexile Code: AD; Lexile Level: 530

978-1-93435-9938 English hardcover ISBN
978-1-60718-0388 English paperback ISBN
978-1-62855-3925 Spanish paperback ISBN
978-1-60718-0586 English eBook downloadable ISBN
978-1-60718-0487 Spanish eBook downloadable ISBN
Interactive, read-aloud eBook featuring selectable English (978-1-60718-2863) and Spanish (978-1-62855-1174) text and audio (web and iPad/tablet based)

Translated into Spanish: ¿Qué es nuevo en el zoológico? Una aventura de suma con los animales

1. Zoo animals--Juvenile literature. 2. Counting--Juvenile literature. 3. Addition--Juvenile literature. 4. Zoo animals. 5. Counting. I. Waites, Joan C. II. Title.

QL77.5 .S52 2009
590.73   2009922604

Printed in China November 2019
This product conforms to CPSIA 2008
4th Printing

Arbordale Publishing
Formerly Sylvan Dell Publishing
Mt. Pleasant, SC 29464
www.ArbordalePublishing.com